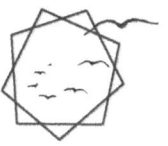

A Tried Heart

A Tried Heart

POETRY AND PROSE POETRY

Raymond C. Mock

A Tried Heart

poems and prose poetry

Copyright ©2017 Raymond C. Mock

ISBN: 978-1-940769-86-8

Publisher: Mercury HeartLink

Silver City, New Mexico

Printed in the United States of America

All rights reserved. This book, or sections of this book, may not be reproduced or transmitted in any form without permission from the author, except for brief quotations embodied in articles, reviews, or used for scholarly purposes.

Permission is granted to educators to create copies of individual poems, with proper credits, for classroom or workshop assignments.

Contact the author at: rcm100@netzero.net

Mercury HeartLink
www.heartlink.com

*for my friends
who asked me
and encouraged me
to share my writing*

Dedication	VII
About this Book	XIV
Acknowledgements	XV

SPRING

Friendship	3
A Star	4
A Pear	5
Sheila	6
Voyager	7
Peggy	8
No Words	9
In Ignorance	10
I'm Not Honest	11
A Lighthouse	12
Art	13
Sunshine	14
Beware the Crowd	15
Gandhi	16
Like a Woman	17
An Ambassador	18
I Look at Skies	19
Reach Far Above	20
Steam Locomotive	21
What Are We Reaching For?	22
Falling in Love	23

So I Can Cry	24
Everyone Does It	25
We Only Had Dinner	26
You Don't Have to Be	27
A Lonely Universe	28
Dresses	29
To Write a Poem	30
A Smile	31
Diane	32
As a Bird	34
Still in Our Youth	35
Rita	36
An Artist	38
April	39
Karen	40
A Lady	41
Your Best Dress	42
The Beauty of Hearts	44
Climbing Hills	46
If Only	47
Things and Woman	48
Crystal Piano	50
Watching the Waterfall	51
She's There	52
I'm Comfortable	54
A Flower	55
My Honesty	56
You	57

SUMMER

A Quality	61
Moon Hung Low	62
The Train Called A Dame	63
The Loveliest Woman	64
I See a Little Girl	65
Not Proposal	66
The Same Heart	68
Committed	69
Magic Wand	70
When Clouds Paint	71

FALL

Suns Mostly Set	75
Silent Talk	76
By Loving Others	78
Sunday Late	79
Endless	80
The Leaves Have Sung	82
Black Leather Dress	83
Pine Trees	84
Through Shaded Window	85
The High Domain	86
Bright Candles	87
Meals Alone	88
Divine Signs	89
Minute, Writing Class	94

Marble	97
A Rockwell	99
Flower of Creation	100
2012 State Fair	102
Silent Din	104
Albuquerque Autumn	106
Poetry Pointed	108
I Let the Dog Out	109
Retaining Wall	110
Spirits Sprite	114
Hearts of the Air	116
High Aqua	118
A Roly-Poly	121
Refuge	122
Prophetic Whisper	124
Winter	125
The Sermon	126
Treasures	128
Insidious Hole	130
Kiss	132
Rocks	133
Consuming	134
Lection	135
For a Tree	136
Marbles	138
A Leaf Falls	139
Destined Observer	140

Angelic Air	141
Doctor Appointment	142
que	143
Abyss	144
Effervescence	146
After	149
ABOUT THE AUTHOR	151

About this Book

A Tried Heart is a collection of best poems and prose presented in the order written. Some works have been revised. Written from heartfelt experience, the book is fundamentally nonfiction.

The book has been divided into **Spring, Summer,** and **Fall** sections to frame the author's lifework to date. But note that some later works represent reflections on earlier events.

Acknowledgements

Thanks to my fellow writers at Wordwright Writing Class and Silk Purse Poets for their artful comments over the years.

Thanks to Jeanne Shannon for her professional review.

Thanks to Stewart Warren for his insight and support.

Spring

Friendship

Friendship is bound
With many consistent and hidden stitches.

A Star

With courtesy, you soothe me.
With honesty, you beckon my trust.
Your independence is a reference,
A star to lift my eye,
A friend in a sky of loneliness.

A Pear

People leave me be
As a pear to rot.

May the seed yield a tree
And feed the lot.

Sheila

Your voice is music.
Your laughter, song.
Your smile is a full rainbow.
Your heart, a rose petal.

Voyager

By a cold craft
Adrift in intrigue,
Man's farthest dreams
Are brought to his feet;
He dreamed of worlds
And set out to see,
Now he gazes
God's laboratory.

Peggy

Each time I see you
Your face is anew
Like the many flowers
I give you.

And my thoughts each day
Build a bright bouquet
Of a woman I like,
A lady too.

No Words

I love
To rendezvous with you—
Seeing your smile and bright eyes
Under golden hair,
Seeing the sway of your walk,
Hearing the song in your voice.

I love
To talk with you—
With your unpredictable ways
That delight me
And your common sense
That wins me.

I love
To think of you—
Filling my breath
With your sensuality,
Longing to touch you
Like no words can do.

In Ignorance

In ignorance
Lies the worst of man,
Giving rise
To basest passions
And worst atrocities.

Only by knowledge
Is a man changed,
Dispelling the harshness
Of his young creed.

I'm Not Honest

I'm not honest
 with you.
When your eyes
 look so lovely,
When your hair
 lies upon your face,
When your body
 speaks its presence,
When your legs
 thrill me,
I should say so.

A Lighthouse

A lighthouse I gave,
Of crystal made,
Easily broken.

In its ruby light
My own heart bright,
Easily broken.

Art

Art is not
What I see,
But observe;

A tree
I draw
Is me.

And sight felt
Is worthy,
So I tell.

Sunshine

Sunshine,

>I want to play
>With your golden rays,
>
>Put my hands
>Upon your sphere,
>
>Cuddle
>To your warmth,
>
>And stay
>In your light.

Sunshine,

>It's hard
>To say good night.

Beware the Crowd

Beware the crowd,
The whole is smaller
Than an individual.

Gandhi

No one is alone—

Each heart
Shares the experience—

We are one.

Like a Woman

Like a woman,
You have shown to me
The beauty in song,
The man in this guy.

Like an angel,
You have shown to me
That spirits are one,
That clouds kiss the sky.

An Ambassador

Each one
Is an ambassador
Of one's kind.

If one lies,
So does one's kind.

If one cheats,
So does one's kind.

For prejudice
Comes from experience,
Not just ignorance.

I Look at Skies

I look at skies
With clouds on air
And see your eyes,
The soul they bear.

Mountains and trees
Touch me through you;
We . . .
Are more than two.

And your body
Calls tenderly.
You . . .
Make life lovely.

Reach Far Above

Reach far above
Your sphere of sight.

Peace lies not here;
Faith take thee far.

Break your shackles;
In truth find flight.

Slay inner fears,
Heal even scars.

Steam Locomotive

Dinosaur of steel,
Dragon of fire
Beating music on the track,
Boasting loud through its stack.

Making a mark
In the hearts of men,
Shaping their minds
Like the tracks they bend.

What Are We Reaching For?

We cover canvas with loving touch,
Carve sculpture both smooth and rough.
What are we reaching for?

We unravel matter, math, and physics,
Uncover the *ah* of natural laws.
What are we reaching for?

We speak the language of the wind,
Sing verse of hearts and ends.
What are we reaching for?

And we find by truth a consenting soul
Willing our arms to hold.
What are we reaching for?

Falling in Love

Falling in love
Is your first music lesson.

So I Can Cry

God,
Reach inside me;
Take my heart,
My soul,
And put them together
In my throat
So I can cry
With love
Till tears cleanse me,
Till purity lets me see.

Everyone Does It

Everyone does it,
So must you.
Right or wrong,
You have to.

Baa-a-a.

We Only Had Dinner

We only had dinner,
But your face was aglow.

Tender eyes did sparkle.
Golden hair moved oh slow.

A moist smile did undress
Teeth pure as river stone.

And moving in your chair,
Angel wing touched my bone.

Like waking to winter's
White beauty so bare.

We only had dinner,
But dessert, we shared.

You Don't Have to Be

You don't have to be
Like other people
And don't have to be
Ignorant of them.

Till thirty, one seeks
One's self in others.
After thirty, one seeks
One's self within.

But you'll never find
A thing of value
Until another
Places love in you.

And when attraction,
Respect, fun come true,
Magic kisses too,
Then you'll unwrap you.

A Lonely Universe

We walk in a sea of beings.
Crowded. Yet within each,
A lonely universe . . .
Waiting, wanting to be discovered,
Hoping to collide with another.

Dresses

Dresses show figures
And hide figures.
I fill in.

Eyes hold me,
Then let go.
I fill in.

Hearts warm me,
Then turn cold.
I fill in.

You woke me
To a dream
Only you fill in.

To Write a Poem

To write a poem
Is to catch a butterfly;

Be vigilant,
Don't chase,
And when it's near,
Cast the net.

Then,
Inhale its beauty
Or exhale mundane.

But each is only one—
A species none.

Until the sharing;
Then it's free,
Destined on winds
Of humanity.

A Smile

A smile,
A common woman
I cannot forget.

Her heart was on her face—
Her lips traced it,
Her eyes lived it,
Her cheeks blushed with it,
She . . . defined it.

Leonardo, I know you;
Mona Lisa was this.
You hoped to hold it
On canvas.

But only nature
Designs such wine
As a woman's smile
On a man's mind.

Diane

Men call many
A woman lovely,
But few are,
As I see.

In a Sunday paper,
A magazine, a picture,
Her loveliness
Captures me.

Her beauty lifts page;
In my mind
She takes stage.
So rare, so sublime.

Hair flows, glows
Like dark wine,
Tenderly curls on tender shoulders.
I tenderly pine.

Her brow
Speaks even now.
Lips poised in her being.
Complexion worthy to keep her.

Eyes holding soul,
Holding my heart;
This picture, this paper,
Tears me apart.

As a Bird

As a bird is shaped
To mate the wind,

As its flight
Is a graceful sight,

As its feather
Can be so tender,

As its song
Does belong,

As its heart
Beats true;

So please me,
You do.

Still in Our Youth

Science is a matter of fact.
Religion, a matter of faith.
Do not judge one by the other,
For it is a fool's endeavor.

And faith cannot judge another;
You are yourself, not your brother.
Free to choose, to think, to believe;
Not to scorn another's belief.

There are bright stars in every sky.
Some not so to the naked eye.
But the sky is continuous,
And so too are our differences.

Knowing this, we can coexist.
We're still in our youth, seeking truth.
Difference is a trait to savor,
Not a cause for hate to sever.

Rita

If you were single,
I'd let you know.
But you're married.
You've places to go.

I get high . . .
Just looking at you.
The moon and Venus
Too soon pass through.

Attractive lady,
I muse your wild soul,
Admire your body
From head to toe.

All things beautiful
In all your part;
Physical attraction,
Essence of art.

Your loveliness,
Adorned with dress.
A woman is right
To be her best.

No angel could
Display more grace
Than this woman's
Most earthly place.

An Artist

An artist
Feeds on emotions;

He uses inspiration
To climb heights

And depression
To forge depths.

He takes us on a journey
Through ourselves;

Our minds,
Memories on shelves,

Our hearts
Know the steps.

April

April,
Like a maple:

>Her hair
>Fills the air,
>
>Her trunk,
>Slim and strong,
>
>Her body,
>Tender leaves throng,
>
>Her legs
>Root into my soul,
>
>Her arms
>Extend her charms.

Come dawn,
She puts color on.

Come eve,
It brightly falls.

Come night,
Her beauty instills delight.

Karen

She is poetry.
We said not hello.
Yet, I know—
Senses told me.

Her lips, petals on a rose.
Her youth, a cool river's flow.
Today, I am old—
Ages told me.

A Lady

I meet lovely women
But look for a lady;
So many a pretty face
Lack that tender grace.

There are many
Portraits out there.
I sense you so strongly,
None compare.

You draw me;
A sunset lovely,
A river wild and free,
Untamable, yet gentle.

A panorama, scenic view
Set vertical in you—
Lips like water, body like earth—
Seeing you, a rebirth.

I've never sensed beauty so deep;
When you move, you flow,
I hear your heart when you speak,
Your body is your soul.

Your Best Dress

Our eyes meet, as they do,
You turn to me, I to you,
And our hearts dance
In a rush of romance.

And so like you
To add to this
Your best dress
Of violet blue.

It's simple, like you.
Cut elegant, like you.
Unique, like you.
Bright, like you.

It displays you
Before me,
Arms and legs bare.
Still, with dignity.

Tenderness,
Loveliness,
Presence,
Beauty.

More than a dress,
More than a woman,
More than my heart
Can express.

The Beauty of Hearts

My heart first broke at ten.
It was older than I
And couldn't deny her.
Friends broke it again.

Then came seventeen.
I loved a pompom queen.
But I kept low,
Couldn't let friends know.

Again at twenty one,
I was still too young.
She played around.
Friends let me down.

But now I'm grown,
On my own, a man;
A woman took my hand
And became my friend.

To touch the fire
And not be consumed,
Sunlit flowers
Having reached full bloom

Is the beauty
Of hearts
Beyond
Bitter starts.

Climbing Hills

Wheels roll along, eighteen strong,
But this load seems a haul too long.
Sometimes it seems life has nothing
To carry on.

This breathing steel pulls up the hill
With a moan not unlike I feel.
Sometimes it seems life is nothing
But climbing hills.

But the clouds remind me of her hair.
Oh, how the sun does shine up there.
I remember her face, just as fair.
And the grass does for me pray
As it kneels upon breast of clay.
I hold myself together, one more day.

A man that roams, a truck his throne,
But no woman to call his own.
Sometimes it seems life gives nothing
When you're alone.

This breathing steel pulls up the hill
With a moan not unlike I feel.
Sometimes it seems life is nothing
But climbing hills.

If Only

I could break water,
    slip the sea,
I could make a wake
    extend eternally
If only you'd fill me
    with your breeze.

Things and Woman

What makes a man love things?
What makes man love woman?
Whatever guides him to her,
He sculpts—metallic, wooden.
A woman is made of parts;
He watches her move them.
A train is made of parts;
He watches steam move them.
A man loves things and woman.
His world is filled by them.

Man gives things feminine names;
He thinks of them like woman.
You see, in his eye,
Things beautiful are feminine.
He makes things with his hands,
Stands over his creation.
She's made by God's hand,
The loveliest creation.
A man loves things and woman.
His world is filled by them.

What makes a man love things?
What makes man love woman?
Whatever guides him to her,
He sculpts—metallic, wooden.
Man loves to control his things.
He takes pride in their being.
He takes pride in a woman
Who controls his very being.
A man loves things and woman.
His world is filled by them.

Crystal Piano

I give to you
A crystal piano
For the sound of beauty
And fond memory
You've given me—
I'm one key of many
You have touched.

Watching the Waterfall

I sat on the plaza
Watching the waterfall.
She strolled in beside it.
Then, sitting at its edge,
She stole its thunder,
Stole my heart beside it.

Her dress deep blue, eyes too,
Hair fell like water.
Her moves made waves;
My heart rose on crests beside her.
I stared. She stared.
Yet, a doubt about her.

So I walked her way,
Unsure the path that lay,
Hoping to be beside her.
But, it passed her by
Knowing I'd be the fool
To sit beside her.

She's There

Your hair, a curl,
Bounces on your forehead,
Pats so caringly.

Your back, as you sit
On a piano bench,
A vase would stare.

Your legs,
Slender to the thick,
Stick in my mind.

Your dress, sleeveless,
Begs me to touch
Shoulders so soft.

Your walk
Slips like a princess.
Your figure, no less.

Your eyes
Touch me tenderly,
Talk to me honestly.

Your voice
Embraces my ear;
Words softer than air.

My heart
Cries
She's there.

I'm Comfortable

I'm comfortable.
I trust you.
I want to spend time with you,
Share your poetry.

I enjoy your company.
I want your friendship.
My heart wants more.
My mind's not sure.

You're lovely to see
And lovelier within.
Trust and friendship will endure.
Of this, I'm sure.

I could carve it in stone
Or on a tree.
Oh hell, I'll just ask you
To coffee.

A Flower

So many a flower
Each its own beauty
So many a woman
Has compelled me

A man's life
Is filled with bloom
His heart
Can find room

But a wise man
Will pick only one
Be not hasty
Nor wait too long

And be he true
She'll not fade—
He her sun
He her shade

My Honesty

I want to give you
The one thing
No other man can,
My honesty.

I couldn't cheat you
Like other men;
I'm not blind
With their sins.

You're the loveliest thing
I've ever seen;
My heart takes wing.

I want you to know me
As God does.
I love you, solely.

You

I look in your eyes
To see you.

I kiss your lips
To kiss you.

I touch your skin
To touch you.

Your body is heavenly,
Yet you . . . move me.

Summer

A Quality

You have a quality
Like no other lady.
It permeates you—
Mind, soul, and body.
It's lovely.

Can you fault me
For seeing your beauty?
It permeates me—
Mind, soul, and body.
You're lovely.

Moon Hung Low

Moon hung low,
Full and yellow,
Embraces the meadow,

Climbs the blue night,
High and white,
In my window's sight.

Touches the child in me,
A memory—
Parents watching over me.

Their love, bright.
My heart, light.
Child, sleep tight.

The Train Called A Dame

Did you ever ride the train,
The train called A Dame?
It's only love, only love again.
The world passes by.
You want to die.
It's only love, love passing by.

It doesn't stop.
You can't get off.
Rocks you on your feet, in your sleep.
Bliss would be if she rode too,
But she wants no part of you.
Love of your life, ride of strife.

Each new love adds a car;
A new experience, more intense.
Yet it's the same, the same old train.
It takes you to a place,
A place you did not choose;
Love lost in a dream, hungering.

Always alone, alone you ride,
Always alone, alone you bide
The train called A Dame.
And a whistle cries in the night,
Some comfort rides beside the pain;
Yours is not the only train.

The Loveliest Woman

You're the loveliest woman
I've ever met.
I want you to know it.

And I want you to know
It hurts to see
And not say you're lovely.

I See a Little Girl

I see a little girl,
Hair in curls,
Wishing upon stars,
Wondering what they are.

Still in curls but grown,
Your heart falls like stone
For no heart has man.
You wonder if he can.

But my love is more
Than mortal man.
My love is whole.
My love is soul.

Destiny should put me
At the side of you
Or make me a star
So your dreams come true.

Not Proposal

Admiration,
When exalted,
Is mistaken
For proposal.

Admiration,
When one lacks soul,
Is reduced to
Proposition.

Not proposal,
Not proposition;
Just poetry
Of your beauty.

My heart is true.
My soul, silver.
You'll never find
A better mirror.

Perhaps someday
Another will hold me;
I'm always drawn
By the lovely.

Not proposal,
Not proposition;
You needn't fear
This poet's mirror.

The Same Heart

I've never been
More in love
Than I am
With you—

Beautiful woman,
Lovely person,
Sweet lady,
Tender memory.

But don't think
I'm sure of myself;
I asked you to coffee
To figure out me.

I want to be
A plus
In your life,
A thought you trust.

Race and age
Set us apart,
But I sense
The same heart.

Committed

Like you,
I'm from the old school.

Loose women
Don't thrill me.
A woman must
Be a lady.

And the lady in you
Is radiant.
Behavior so beautiful,
I didn't know.

You opened a door
I can't back through.
I'm committed
To loving you.

Magic Wand

Home,
Where gardens grow,
Pets lie content,
Children stand tall.

And all
From the touch of a hand,
The magic wand
Of a mom.

When Clouds Paint

Red clouds above blue,
Silver lining between the two,
Sandia Mountains bear their name
As when the Spaniards came.

Clouds like ice
Cast mountains in blue,
Beverage for the eyes.
The drink, cool.

Where two clouds cusp,
A holy cross,
Bright, straight, corners square.
My mind still stares.

When clouds paint
Bolder than dreams,
I sense possibility
In human things.

FALL

Suns Mostly Set

Suns mostly set,
Women seem just born,
I remember pets,
Shoes are mostly worn—

Backside of forty-five,
One after one,
Things are numbered now,
To the last one.

I watch TV with Dad.
He's asleep in his chair.
I look at his worn shoes,
And I'm thankful he's there.

Silent Talk

Twin bed,
Chest of drawers,
Books, desk,
Framed awards,

World globe,
Girly calendar,
State map,
Einstein poster,

And a green,
Three by four
Chalk board—
Atypical room.

A window
With mountain view
Is mostly drawn
For solitude.

Luminous script
Of white chalk
Reflects a world
Of silent talk—

Poetry
Pre-penned,
Vector analysis
Neatly handed in,

Chemistry,
Physics,
Electronics,
Art.

Erased now,
The room is dim,
But the board whispers
Of places been.

By Loving Others

By loving others,
One loves oneself.
By gaining knowledge,
One learns oneself.

One without heart,
One without mind
Is one less
God shall find.

For one must strive
To retain on earth
What God did give
At birth.

Sunday Late

Sunday late,
Winds are restless,
Clouds heavy and blue,
Mountains rise with sunset,
Crags of shadow fill my eyes,
And I still have laundry to do.

Endless

Her hair,
Her eyes,
Her nose,
Her lip,
Where lip meets lip,
Her shoulder,
Her arm,
Her small hand,

Her breast,
Where breast meets breast,
Where breast meets side,
Where breast meets child,
Her rib,
Her stomach,
Where stomach meets rib,
Her small waist,

Where hip and leg
Draw the feminine curve,
Her abdomen,
Her thigh,
Her inner thigh,
Where thigh meets thigh,
Her calf,
Her small foot,

And her heart,
Her endless heart,
Where heart meets heart.

The Leaves Have Sung

The leaves have sung
Their dying song,
Black birds on bare branches
An eerie Christmas tree,
The sun cast down
Upon the horizon,
Gray clouds slowly
Bury me—

I sip
My warm honey tea.

Black Leather Dress

Black leather dress,
Impediment,
Hot and heavy.

Her soft finesse
Commands it,
Hot and heavy.

Pine Trees

Pine trees
Cheer in the breeze
With pompoms of spears.

I recall Ann,
Pompoms in hand,
Her beauty speared.

Through Shaded Window

The Moon clears the dark edge
And reflects across the ripple,
But my heart reflects sadness,
Moonlight through shaded window.

The High Domain

Grab the air,
Again and again;
The ground descends.

Now stroke the sky,
Sense the wing,
Befriend the wind.

Lift one wing, raise tail,
Gently tilt the earth;
Control, rebirth.

The high domain;
Patience and training
Grant this blessing.

Now cease the effort
And descend,
Say goodbye to the wind,

Give one long embrace,
And step from the wing
With one last cling.

Bright Candles

Bright candles dot evening,
Gather hearts with flames of joy,
Keep life's merriment near,
Prepare, quiet, resound souls,
And usher vibrantly
The yearly zeal; it's Xmas.

Meals Alone

Beto's, number six, green,
Sunlight takes the chair.

Copper Canyon, coffee and pie,
Silhouettes weave the shade.

Dion's, pepperoni slice,
Wet streets catch the glare.

Meals alone dine on senses,
Taste light, God's salient maid.

Divine Signs

I was in the beginner's Foundation class at church when a lady commented that God doesn't talk to people anymore. I said, "Well, we do have Bibles now, and He may not talk to us but He does give us signs." So I shared my signs with the class.

The first sign was—don't laugh—green lights all the way home. Yes, I asked God for green lights all the way home. I know, it sounds small—you don't ask God for this kind of thing. But some days when I had finished work, I'd feel so tired driving home that I just wanted to fall over on the car seat and go to sleep. I had read the Bible, and although I wasn't a Christian at the time, I strongly sensed that He'd do it. I pointed through the upper windshield and said, "I know you're there, God. I know you're there." Yet, I questioned the experience afterward.

The second sign was, again, green lights all the way home. It was about two weeks after the first sign. But this time I thought about it after asking for green lights and said, "Never mind, God. You have better things to do." Then I thought about it again and said, "You're going to do it anyway, aren't You? You're going to prove Yourself to me, aren't You?" I didn't question the experience this time.

About two weeks after the second sign, a third sign appeared. I didn't ask for this one. Again, I was driving home from work—5 p.m., that's the magic hour. I was driving north on Wyoming. I had passed Central and the next light and was now headed for Lomas. To my left, above Albuquerque's valley, along the Rio Grande, I noticed a cloud stretched north and south with a hole cut into it, a clean cut, a round and straight tunnel. The clouds on the tunnel wall were rotating. I didn't see the clouds rotating, but they were swept around the inner wall as if they had been.

I glanced at the traffic, then looked at the cloud again. At the back of the tunnel, the sun was flashing small bits of light through the back of the cloud. Not lots of bits at once, but one at a time in quick succession, here and there. I didn't think much of it at the time, but I do now. Imagine: the sun, the tunnel, and I were aligned.

I glanced at the traffic again and returned to the cloud. The sun continued flashing through.

Again, I checked the traffic and returned to the cloud. To my surprise, a brilliant cross of golden light with yellow highlights hung before the hole in the cloud. As I glanced over my left shoulder, I said, "Look . . . at . . . that!" My voice was high-pitched, more so with each word. I questioned my sanity: *I'm here, it's there. I'm here, it's there. It's real.*

The cross was perfect. It looked solid and heavy. It was about four times the size of the sun in height. Well, at least three times the size of the sun. It was straight, square, and symmetrical. It had a definite width to its beams, and the ends of the beams were cut square, giving corners.

I wanted to pull over and watch, but my truck was a raft on a river of traffic, carried along by bumpers and doors between banks of curb. I was concerned an accident would occur if drivers were looking at the cross. I expected them to slow down or to stop and look. They didn't. I glanced at the driver in front; he wasn't looking at the cross. I glanced in the rearview mirror at the driver behind; she wasn't looking at the cross. I said, "Nuts with you guys. I'm looking."

The surprise continued, the clouds behind the cross became brighter and brighter, sunbeams streamed in every direction from behind the cross, and the hole became a halo. Squinting, I watched the right arm of the cross to see if it would disappear into the brightness, but the cross was still visible. Then I checked the traffic again, and when I looked back to see the cross, it was gone. All of it, gone.

Now as the river of traffic slowed, stiff-armed by a red light at Lomas, I glanced twice again over my left shoulder. Yes, gone. One second my eyes beheld a magnificent cross and the next a red light stared at me.

Having shared my signs with the class, I looked at each student in turn with my hands out in anticipation of hearing their signs. They shook their heads at me, and the instructor stared like a red light.

After seeing the cross, I thought most of Albuquerque had seen it. I thought it would be on the news. With excitement I drove home, rushed through my apartment door, and turned on the TV. Not a word about the cross. *It'll be on the weather.* No word. I changed the channels, but there was no word about the cross. When I went to work the next day, there wasn't a word. And oddly, I didn't say a word.

I'm a Christian now, but it took more than these signs to bring me to Christ. I once confided in a friend when I was having doubts about my faith; I said, "Maybe God intended that cross for somebody else, and I just happened to see it." She said, "He gave you the green lights, didn't He?" Her words embraced me. And how right she was; the probability of eighteen green lights, one way, five days a week, is about once in a thousand years.

But why show me a cross? Surely, it was instruction to include Christ in my life. But as I've grown in faith, I've come to a simple reflection: God doesn't just answer prayers; if one shows God faith, then God gives blessings.

Lately, recalling details, I've reconstructed a picture of the cross. There were yellow lines that ran the length of the beams, but not to the ends. It was a fine, smaller cross upon the cross. And the yellow highlights extended from the yellow lines toward one edge of the beams. Each highlight was a spot of random shape that gleamed and danced—the cross seemed alive.

Like a branding iron, that cross marked me; it's in my mind, brilliant and perfect. It tells me that when one gets to heaven, one will not believe the light show and will stand there for an eternity saying it's perfect.

But for now, each day God grants, one should read, pray, and grow, or at least park one's hat in Christ's church once a week. And if I may suggest, come 5 p.m., look west.

Minute, Writing Class

The class began with Marsha reading two articles on the semicolon. First, she read the blunt-fisted assault on it, and then the artfully endearing praise. I was glad to have heard both.

Next, Dennis conducted his reading and discussion of professional verse. But despite my comment, I noticed I was laid-back. It seemed I'd coast through this class without much engagement.

Then the class trio began with Janet. She shared her story of character perseverance over emotional rent of family fabric, premature loss of innocence, and the coldness of first independence.

Second was Bob. It wasn't long before he was throwing verbal grenades in his kitchen experience, creating abstract images: natural gas explosions both in-your-face and out of sorry bowels, an accidental yet stable inverted posture, a post-death experience, and a face with anti-makeup. To my surprise, the class reinforced some of these unnatural phenomena.

And last, I experienced the undulating verbiage of Max. Wave upon wave of adjectives drowned his pathetic subject, a man of subhuman nature. Yet, I identified. No, this can't be. And Max continued relentlessly opening my wounds with this suffering creature: it couldn't speak, it would look in from the outside, pine for its beautiful obsession, and observe the lovely people in their happy erotic state. It hurt.

It is. It's me. Fourth grade, I fell for a cute brunette. But she was the smartest girl in school, and I was the dumbest boy, a poor reader. I had an inferiority complex. Then in junior high, she went on the class oversea trip. I sat in history class with the lights out, watching the trip slides. There she was on the screen, drying dishes in the galley. It hurt.

Then, in high school, I fell in love with a pompom queen, a cute brunette, popular, and I, a wallflower. I sat on the gymnasium bleachers watching her on the floor during assembly. A tilt of her hip and a spear went through my heart. I nearly fell from the bleachers. She'd giggle and laugh with her boyfriend on the school plaza at lunch time. I sat beside her in typing class and couldn't speak a word. Her father was a sports broadcaster on a local TV channel. He had his family on TV at Christmas. There she was, wishing people a merry Christmas. Again, it hurt.

Then at twenty-one, I had my first date and first kiss. What a kiss! Yes, she was a cute brunette. Yes, I was in love. But she was an experienced woman, and I was still an introvert. Then she went to work at a bank. They made a commercial. Yes, she was on TV, smiling. Yes, it hurt.

And later, the fourth-grade girl became a pediatrician at a local hospital. The hospital made a commercial, and though she didn't look like the fourth-grade girl, still it hurt.

Thrice impaled, haunted by the TV, and now Max exhumes me. And looming, the letters with poems I mailed to two celebrities, brunettes. Is the unexpected typically ugly?

The class ended. Nearly bled-out, I complimented Max on his *fine* work and exited. *I'm out. I'm safe. I can go home.*

But no, I left the class mind-bent by emotional rent, concussion, and self-exposure. With post-traumatic stress, I drove, waiting for the mental dents to pop out. I was next to the curb when a gauntlet of evergreens, like curled pythons in green camouflage, reached for me, thick, limbs licking. In turn, each sprang over the wall and low to the ground.

Shaken, I pulled in at Dunkin' Donuts. "Coffee. Coffee."

Marble

After picking up groceries late Sunday night, I decided to swing by the pharmacy before driving home. My severance payments had ended, and so too my medical coverage. With depleting medications each day, the personal cost loomed ever larger.

When I approached the counter, there was one customer at the counter and another at the drive-through. I viewed the pharmacist from her side as she handled the drive-through. Her glance spoke calm. She wasn't young or old. Her hair was light in color and had a chiseled do. Her nose was prominent, official, like her white coat.

She approached and asked, "How may I help you?"

I explained my predicament. She walked to the computer, away from the counter, telling me I'd need to speak up so she could hear me. After two attempts to speak my name loudly, I pulled out my driver's license. She looked up the meds. I asked for a monthly price. She said the reflux would cost $174.00 a month. I repeated the price in question.

She walked up to me whispering, "You can buy it on the shelf. I'll show you." I followed her with surprise. There it was, 28 capsules, for $15.00. "Try it," she said, and we went back to the pharmacy. She looked up the other med, $45.00 a month.

"That's not bad," I said.

"No," she replied as she returned my driver's license.

As I took the license, it hit me, in all respects, what a lovely lady. Her face wore a radiance and smoothness. She filled the room like decor. I left the pharmacy with a new breath and solace, enamored, like visiting the Washington monuments.

Later that evening, I caught "American Masters" on TV. It was a documentary on Marilyn Monroe, her photographers, and their personal experiences. One photographer said that the stills caught her best. Another said that her presence placed everything in slow motion.

I watched the stills go by in succession; like being in shock—snap the moment, turn inward for reflection, and then snap another—it created a slow motion. With each image, I caught a better view: yes . . . I see . . . that's her . . . I know her. Each image was bright, breathtaking, magical, the perfect snapshot. Like marble, the photos revealed the Master's work—each curve elegant, prominent, bigger than life, and best framed in white, dress or mattress, like visiting the Washington monuments.

That night, I twice glimpsed the light: angelic souls.

A Rockwell

Black mother and daughter,
White mother and daughter
Sat back to back
At Village Inn.

Mothers sat proper,
But the daughters
Heads turned
To each other.

They stared
In wonder,
Long.
As long as I.

Black daughter
In blue dress,
Blue bows
On pigtails.

White daughter
In pink dress,
Pink ribbon
On ponytail.

A picture
In grey-matter frame.
A Rockwell.
I sign my name.

Flower of Creation

Man grows older,
The mystery grows deeper,
The heart grows warmer.

★ ★ ★

Flower of creation,
God's culmination.
Man kneels at her womb.

Center of the universe,
She knows all songs,
Knows the words.

Listen as she sings,
All good words,
All good things.

Her hair, wind.
Her stare snares,
Then turns away.

Vessel feminine
Crafted for man,
Filled with love.

Bigger than life:
Statue, Meteor, Goddess,
Petite dress.

No lovelier color, eclipse.
No sweeter taste, lips.
No greater flood, love.

In his hand,
A petal's caress.
He falls like sand.

2012 State Fair

I went to the fair
To cruise the art.
Nothing there
I'd take home.

At the hobby show,
The woodcarver's table,
Children pranced
With little owls.

I spotted him
Engraving
Pre-cut owls
With a hot pen,

But walked away,
Mind and heart arguing.
My heart won;
Turn around.

I'll pay you
For one of them.
Well, they're giveaways
For the children.

I've looked around
At this fair;
It's the only thing
I'd take home.

Really? Take one.
There were many.
Choosing, I felt silly,
Picked a solemn one.

Then I went
To the Asbury Café
For coffee and pie.
I ordered and sat.

A young woman
Stood before me.
My eyes were drawn
Toward the ground.

Spurs!
My heart purred.
Asterisk,
Footnote: *feminine*.

I've looked around
At this fair;
She's the only thing
I'd take home.

Glancing now
At that solemn owl,
My breath stirs,
Woman with spurs.

Silent Din

I sat
In church.
She stood
Before me.

Her figure
Flowed
Like a
Waterfall.

Her earth
Danced
Beneath
The eddies.

My heart
Fell in.
Rapids.
Silent din.

Her beauty,
Tsunami.
Debacle
Beat me.

When Beauty
Says hello,
I turn to
Dust.

I sat
In church.
The sermon,
Lust.

Albuquerque Autumn

Blue sky,
Awash in light.
Black highways
Gleam like shores.

Overpasses fly,
Gull wings.
Train tracks,
Whitecaps.

Buildings squat
Like sunbathers.
People meander
Like crabs.

Tall glass buildings,
Like tall ships,
Sail color;
Trees splash, yards drift.

The tide turns;
A cool swell.
East, Watermelon high.
West, crimson veil.

Eve, Night's bosom,
Heaven's children.
Luminous valley,
Sleeping Beauty.

The Moon
Slips to bed.
The stars
Cast dreams.

Poetry Pointed

Poetry pointed,
Pierce my heart
With truth.

In your arms,
Let me die—
Purged by ruth.

Resurrect me
Content,
Beautiful breath.

I Let the Dog Out

I let the dog out.
The moonlight
Surprised me.

O God,
It's beautiful.
But it pangs me.

I yearn
To share
The beauty.

Retaining Wall

The wife wanted
A retaining wall,
A level heaven
Of lawn and garden.
I bought thirty blocks.

Big red blocks,
Lovely.
Stacking seemed easy,
Just thwart the slope.
Bought thirty more blocks.

I read self-help,
Then read again,
Consulted a pro,
Called a friend.
Bought thirty more blocks.

The criteria:
No holes for those
Filthy roaches,
But water must flow.
Bought thirty more blocks.

A perfectionist,
I rejected
The expert's lip—
Criteria unmet.
Bought thirty more blocks.

Bought tools:
Masks, gloves, goggles,
Chisels, hammer, mallet.
Receipts invaded my wallet.
Bought thirty more blocks.

Hoping a plan
Would jump in,
I began
At the deepest end.
Bought thirty more blocks.

The battle waged.
Blocks fallen, I prayed,
"God, show me
How this wall is made."
Bought thirty more blocks.

Fall back, tear it down,
Kill the roaches
In their dens.
Start again.
Bought thirty more blocks.

I dug a trench,
Laid blocks at level's end,
Leveled each from each,
Stacked some to breach.
Bought thirty more blocks.

Then, dug deeper,
Poured dry mortar,
Re-laid blocks
Edge to edge.
Bought thirty more blocks.

The foundation ready,
I sprayed water lightly.
Prayed the mortar to set.
Prayed the mortar to set.
Bought thirty more blocks.

Foundation done,
The battle swung—
Blocks must be backfilled,
Dirt must be checked.
Bought thirty more blocks.

I cut landscape material,
Folded, experimented
Till properly seated
Between the blocks.
Bought thirty more blocks.

I backfilled with dirt,
Filled each cleft.
Then entombed—
Each block a pyramid.
Bought thirty more blocks.

Progress,
Higher.
But the wife would chime,
"We need to go!"
Bought thirty more blocks.

Progress,
Higher.
Thunders threat,
Monsoons broke.
Bought thirty more blocks.

Five hundred and ten blocks,
The wall took breath.
But a wall needs steps.
I read self-help,
Then read again.

Spirits Sprite

Two young ladies,
Spirits sprite,
Suddenly appeared;
A friendship bright.

They embraced.
A dance, their walk.
They exchanged hearts,
Laughter, and talk.

Each fourteen,
Cherub faces.
The church café,
Their fairyland.

Fairies, apparently,
Wear dark jeans
And don white mufflers
To spell winters.

The taller
Had long locks spun
Of golden brown
Kissed of sun,

A brown leather coat
With cloud for collar,
And short brown boots
With frets of glitter.

The other, long dark hair
That blotted light,
And her leathers were cut
From a moonlit night.

Then a pixie appeared,
Age thirteen.
Her slippers whispered
Ballerina.

Her shiny red tee
Broke her black apparel
Like red dawn.
Her smile completed her.

They embraced.
Now, a dance of three.
They were celebrating
Their new wings.

Hearts of the Air

Man's heart wept
Within its cage;
The black bird
Reined the sky.

Then two brothers
Searched their hearts,
Fashioned a kite
For a glide.

They gave it life,
A wind its own.
Man's heart and mind,
The machine's flair.

Ah, kindred of
The firmament,
Black bird and they,
Hearts of the air.

They taught
Others to fly,
But the hawks
Killed so many.

One young loner
So loved the wing
That his machine
Flew the sea.

Knights took rein
On silver steeds,
Flew the winds
Of chivalry.

And the Mustang's
Majestic stride
Lept the wind
Fast as any.

Now, above the clouds
The white arrow flies,
Tip, silver craft,
Feather, vapor.

Humbly I pray,
Hearts fly someday
Betwixt the stars.
Oh, what flies there?

High Aqua

Sand flows,
Waves grow
To the sky,
A mile, shy.

It crests,
Then rests
As rock;
Time balks.

Now, generations
Set time's canter
As Albuquerque,
City, desert flower,

And the Rio Grande,
River, surveyor,
Pay homage:
Sandia Mountains.

Its mane
Reigns.
Its breast,
Breath.

North,
The face, stubble,
Five o'clock
Shadow.

Its arm,
Biceps,
Lays fist
Down.

South,
The breast,
The forest
Suckles.

Its arm
Yearns
To tend
Four Hills.

The flow
Now shows
In rolling
Evergreens.

The sun's
Glitter
Now reflects
In aspens.

Its heart
Heavy,
Tears flow
In streams.

Clouds visit,
Remind it
That time
Will find it.

In winter
It braces,
Its backbone
White.

On cloudy days,
Sun breaks,
Light gates
High aqua:

Color, Heaven,
A door open.
My heart
Pants.

A Roly-Poly

I spotted a roly-poly
Crawling around in circles.
I wondered if he knew.

He was on the linoleum.
Normally I'd kill him,
But I let him go.

No . . . not circles,
Progressive loops,
Effective . . . efficient hunting.

Does a bug know something?
Has he been schooled?
I wondered if he knew.

Refuge

My dog stands square
Like a piggy bank:
No life, no money,

Waiting, eyes staring
For the slightest penny.
I check the clock—

He runs for his leash.
The weather, cool, cloudy.
The snow, patchy.

At the park,
People walk their dogs.
My Terrier, different:

His thin frame
Sweeps the leash,
A kite with short tail,

Flying about,
Biting the grass,
His wind within.

I seek refuge
In a quiet thick
Of pine and ash.

Standing on ground
That an Ash stands in,
My attention, courted.

Below me,
Roots of age
Serve with solemn.

Above me,
Large limbs
Draw to veins.

Gray clouds bow,
Snow kneels humbly,
The Ash embraces all.

All is calm—one.
We'll visit again,
Tomorrow.

Prophetic Whisper

I woke early and couldn't sleep.
I dressed and headed east for breakfast.
The clouds covered the mountain peaks.
The morning bore a dark grey cast.

But south of the mountain, in high valley,
A brilliant light shown in the mist,
Iceberg of vapor, prophetic whisper.
I ordered breakfast and sat for the Feast.

A gray mist beset the entire city,
But a white globe hung in the east.
The mist brewed into gnarly teeth,
Surrounded, and chewed it to pieces.

Snowflakes fell like fine crumbs,
The sky grew darker, the day lost color,
Depression won, and crumbs blew strong;
But I embraced the prophetic whisper.

Then, a gray glow grew, drew its arms,
So bright, I couldn't stare. The mist relented
With open mouth; red lips released the sun.
Before I woke, this day was drawn.

Winter

Frozen blanket alights,
Like night but white.
Cold sheets preceded
With crows imprinted.

Above, sky, canvas,
Wintry trees, sketches.
But streets turn to messes,
And the cold depresses.

Winter overstays:
Fireplaces fray,
Incenses embark,
Embers refuge in hearts.

The Sermon

As I approached
The church,
The season
Embraced me.

In the fountain,
Cherry blossoms
Were floating
Like islands.

Tender,
They clustered
In the arms
Of corners.

Away,
The waterfall
Awaited
Them all.

In church,
Voices sang
Just as loud
In the back.

The sermon
Reverbed
Beneath
The roof.

But beneath
The sky I head
The sermon
Of blossoms.

Treasures

At family dinners,
Topics turn crude.
Sister asks, "Where's *your* funny hairs?"
I answer, "On my ears."
Dad speaks, "That's funny!"

A young girl spins,
Her arms
And white dress spread.
I point.
"Look at the snow flake."

A man sits for lunch,
His baby beside him.
I comment,
"You have the mother lode today."
He smiles a mouthful.

A young woman signs.
Her mother smiles
And signs back.
I feel the felt,
A mother's love.

Dad's getting old,
He confides in me.
"Did you ever blow your nose
And have a big—"
"Dad, please, we're not *that* close."

When you're older,
Gifts are gifts,
But
Moments together
Are treasures.

Insidious Hole

Coffee cold,
Senses bewildered.

From the kitchen nook,
I look upon the day.

The wife discerns.
"What's wrong?"

I view life
From a grave.

    Enter the angel,
    Lovely doctor, white coat.

    "How do you feel?"
    "Buried, dead."

    She draws near.
    "You're not going to . . ."

    I query me.
    "No, not yet."

        Depression,
        Insidious hole,

Loneliness, despair,
The mind cannot stay.

Buried in your head,
Reboot—med.

The option
Beseeches your clay.

Kiss

Essence
Stirs,
Reverence
Stills.

Breath
Anticipates,
Heart
Quakes.

Eyes listen,
Lips pose—
Beckon
Of the rose.

Lips touch,
Suspend,
Press,
Passion—

Breath
For two,
Ice and fire
Consume.

Rocks

Rocks, crags,
Mountains—
Stoic, cleric,
Podiums.

Rocks, spherules,
River stones—
Oh current,
Spirit, repose.

Mountains
Attest sermons.
River stones
Avow baptisms.

Consuming

The mountains,
Signs.
Crevices,
Inscriptions.

The river,
Pilgrim,
Parade
Of motion.

I sit
On a tailgate,
Consuming Coke, hotdog,
And landscape.

For a moment—
Bone and skin
Will not
Outlive them.

But in spirit
I'll mourn their end.
I think I'll be sad
In Heaven.

LECTION

At the dental office,
A little girl walks in circles
Around the center table.

She stops and smiles.
I smile.
She smiles. I smile.

She makes circles again—
We wind
Each other's spring.

For a Tree

Incoming
Adrenalin
Hold on
The road again

I turn back
Searching
For something
Imposing

A pine tree
Tall, full, green
Roots embracing
Ground swelling

I look for
Its compliment
My heart
Wrecks

A dreary house
Door weathered
Chimney leaning
Drapes tattered

A small lot
Cracked drive
Grass, what's left
Barely alive

Wood fence broken
Rock wall fallen
A home rich
For a tree

Marbles

Digging crabgrass,
I find marbles
I'd thought were gone.

Looking at the sky,
I see myself
In one.

And at night,
The cosmic glass
Is filled with them.

Surprises
Find
The kid again.

A Leaf Falls

Standing in a park
Beneath a tree,

A leaf falls
In front of me.

Small things
Speak loudly.

Life is a season,
The next, eternity.

Destined Observer

Each day like yesterday.
Tomorrow never comes.

Years settle into dust.
Dreams become crumbs.

Can't escape loneliness.
Can't trust a lover.

Can't drown thirst.
Can't sate hunger.

Heartbeat stilled.
Destined observer.

Angelic Air

Driving to church, I anticipate.

The radio plays an unfamiliar tune.

Piano, a solo, note after tender note.

As I park, angelic air pierces my heart.

And as I walk, a red sun takes stage on the horizon.

I turn to witness the mountains, but the moon surprises me.

Nested atop the trees, it sits solemn in the balcony.

High, a white cloud with billowed crown whispers majesty.

And now, the mountains witness me.

Nature bows, God's will, glory.

I should pray on my knees.

Doctor Appointment

Primary doctor
In evening dress,

Chiffon, light pink,
She its breath.

Professional visit,
I fail to compliment.

We discuss treatment,
I glance, acknowledgment.

Her smile, a crescent.
Her glow, a flower.

Appointment, Princess,
On memory's altar.

QUE

I wrote a poem
With the word *intrigue*,
Placed it on a photo
For friends to keep.

But inadvertently
Placed a *q* for *g*.
I hope it stays
In Albuquerque.

Abyss

My wife and I
Consult a doctor.

The doctor begins,
"Mastectomy."
"No," my wife replies.
"You'll die."
"No!"

Discord, abyss—
My resolve slips.

* * *

I find myself
On a mountain,
Climbing alone
Near the peak.

A dark cloud
Descends,
Dims the light,
Isolates me—

I don't want to be here.
I don't want to be here!

* * *

I awake beside her . . .
And take her hand.

Effervescence

I search the bookstore for a Christian magazine but find nothing of interest. *I'm here, what else can I look for? ... Poetry.* But the poetry section is not where I remember it.

A young lady leaves her portable bookrack at the end of the aisle and approaches me. "Can I help you find something?"

Pointing my right thumb to the side, I ask, "Poetry is probably on the next aisle?"

She points above and behind herself and says, "No, we moved it upstairs. You can take the escalator up—careful, it's not working. Turn right at the top, walk halfway down the aisle, yeah yeah."

I say, "OK," and pass by her. But a distraction lingers: *Yeah yeah, did she say yeah yeah?* And yet, behind her words, there was an energy, an effervescence that clung to me.

There were signs on each side of the escalator: OUT OF ORDER, PLEASE CLIMB STEPS. I start to climb but find myself marching as the first few steps are not raised far. I feel silly and hope no one has seen me.

The poetry books are limited to two small sections no higher than my eyes. Each book I find has long poems.

I hate long poems. I pull some thinner books from the shelf. Long poems again. I tire of the poetry. Her short words return to me: *yeah yeah.* And my lungs inhale quickly as if to nudge me.

Going down the working escalator, I reconsider the distraction: *Where is she? There, the next aisle over, far end.* But: *What am I doing? I never really saw her face. I wouldn't recognize her without her bookrack.* Mission: talk to her, tap her effervescence.

As I approach her, she asks, "Did you not find it?"

"No, I found it. It's a small section. Just as well though, the poems are too long; if poets have something to say, they should get to the point. The best words I've heard all night were yeah yeah."

"I knew when I said that," she says. Her fingers press to her forehead, her head goes back, and her eyes close. "I don't know why I . . ." Her head drops as her fingers now spread across her head. This was effervescence of another sort. We were both in shock, she from me, I from her, like two rail cars coupling hard, shuddering.

Inadvertently, I step toward her and press my finger into her upper arm. I stare at my finger, carefully gaging the depth of depression, and say, "No, it was lovely, I loved it." But I feel like a choirboy stumbling into confession, questioning new boundary. Then a fear: *Did I just assault her?* I say, "Goodbye," and quickly turn the corner of the aisle.

Her voice follows. "Goodbye."

I find myself moving efficiently to the exit as if on a conveyor. I look around the store to gain perspective: *Yep, I'm leaving.*

Outside, I stop. *That was awkward . . . but lovely.*

After

After the darkest night
Comes the softest light.

About the Author

Born in Denver, Colorado, Mid-1950, Raymond C. Mock grew up in Albuquerque, New Mexico beginning in late 1950. An electronic technician by trade, he has written poetry since the 1980s. He has published one poem, "A Smile," in *The Promise of Tomorrow* by The National Library of Poetry in 1997 and again that year by the same publisher in *A Celebration of Poets: Showcase Edition*.

Additionally, four of his poems, "Sunday Late," "Albuquerque Autumn," "Silent Din," and "Falling in Love," were published in *Muse with Blue Apples, an anthology of the New Mexico Poetry Alliance*, by Mercury HeartLink in 2016.

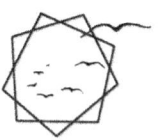

www.ingramcontent.com/pod-product-compliance
Lightning Source LLC
Chambersburg PA
CBHW051651040426
42446CB00009B/1077